WHEN I WAKE IT WILL BE
FOREVER

Sundress Publications • Knoxville, TN

Editor: Erin Elizabeth Smith
erin@sundresspublications.com
http://www.sundresspublications.com

Colophon: This book is set in Palatino and Adobe Garamond Pro.

Cover Design: Mary Ellen Knight

Cover Image: "Tulips" by Gloria Kimmet

Book Design: Erin Elizabeth Smith

Author Photo: Phil Rice

WHEN I WAKE IT WILL BE FOREVER

Virginia Smith Rice

ACKNOWLEDGEMENTS

Grateful acknowledgment is made to the editors of the following publications where these poems and parts of poems have appeared, some in slightly different versions: *2River View, Denver Quarterly, The Jet Fuel Review, Lily Review, Moria, Rattle, Southern Poetry Review, Stirring: A Literary Collection, Stone Highway Review, Superstition Review,* and *Weave.*

Many thanks to Reg Gibbons, Simone Muench, and Ed Roberson, whose guidance and support helped build the foundation for this collection. Thanks also to Aaron DeLee, C. Russell Price, and Christine Pacyk for their critical feedback, and to Lana Rakhman and Kellen Fisher for their willingness to act as 'front line' readers in the development of this collection.

Special thanks to Gene Kimmet for his unfailing generosity, patience, and sense of humor over the years, and for his invaluable insight on all things poetic. It has been a wonderful conversation.

For Gene and Gloria
who taught me how
to live in both worlds.

CONTENTS

I.

II.

III. Curiosity Boxes

IV.

Night holds our breath and lets the story
be, as stories are always wanting to be,

offering us damp palms, pearled brows
and lips, all those wet, open-mouth kisses.

I

Comes an I without
words. Comes an I

who sees a world
end and builds an

other, from voice
missing the silence.

[tell me more about this dragging]

Listen: a roof strafed
and bruised silence after

and no one's death required,
only a slow, singular un-

sexing. Or was it sudden?
Memory the real casualty,

causality chained to a locket
that charms the trees, gold

and galled, blistered evenings
difficult to fill, a dog's jaw

circling a wrist. *Remember*
remember – centipede scars

from an abrupt brisance,
shattered white tarping cars

and street and all the houses.
Call it millefiori-brilliant:

a thunderous, percussed absence
that still cuts and hums

through broken sleep
lit by inner, hidden suns.

[*whose tight-fisted little tyrant are you?*]

Black-pearled tongue uncoils
  at the root, loosens tail from teeth and
         spiders up

a dust-red throat: voice thorned and singing
  but not human.

At no point do we speak to one another: you

a face painted on the ground, marred by crumbled
  dull silver: a figure kneeling among

crushed stalks in violet autumn light: copper
  green-bristled wings covering the sun.

  No longer green-
 scented but vast, a forest breaks through earth
       and believes it is the world.

Wind leafs through branches, hissing almost
  a word: mouth closed, now open.

Sky drags over the forest crown, pressing
  bent edges light cannot
       enter: two bodies

  faced with one another that open
and open while inside a smooth yellow seed closes
       gently, with a click.

[*about bats*]

I don't understand bats, why they loop
over my head at dusk, but some details stay

just as remembered, and how often
     can you say that?

Night after night, stepping into a house
flush with anger, stubble-coarse,
that gives way at last to silence – still angry,

but without words, which makes us less
human with one another, and bearable.

I tried spinning out of one life and the bats
     moved with me,
papering space with odd sightings: a black sock

crumpled in the washer, scooped out before
I feel tiny bones or see the bared teeth:

     another perched, twitching
my pillow at dawn as I stir   startle   freeze.

     Most trap themselves
inside at night: like an infant's hunger
or the croup, the timing is their own,

with nothing to do but stumble out of bed
     and answer to them.

It is possible to develop a competence
at anything, even trapping a small, clicking fright

latched to a curtain, aiming heavy towels
    away from the clean

dishes stacked in the drainer: fold
the fabric quickly underneath, run to the door
and fling the whole bundle out.

    It is difficult
to hold still and discover anything

new in the day. Bats know this:
that's why they are most alive in the dark.

[*a world scarcely the size of an apple*]: *a cento*

Married life
embedded with something that wants
to cause it slight harm: black roots

threading fingernails and shoes,
the endless scent of onions and olive oil,

stone hands filled with vinegar, voice
shaped only by things.

How threatening become the names
of months, cut violets and curtains,

the sharp damp of leaves accustomed
to earth and exasperated winter.

Peace to you, dark sun,
and to you, blind brow.

I want to reach calamity and not be
carried off slowly by blue beetles
and devouring vines.

Sometimes skin flames like a coin
through my fingers: I want the clear day

of your legs, abandoned orange-
blossom wind and what spins between
its gold claws

as twilight goes on erasing statues,
chasing vanished things, vanished beings.

[*the tree across the street*]

You look out the window, say *I'm leaving.*
    All right, I answer – all right for you to go

and you do, a mark left where your hand
    pressed against glass. I look through it to the tree

across the street, studying the nearest branch
    filled with blue-green leaves, those on the far side

lit yellow – one tree caught in two moments
    of light, broken when I realize light and tree

no longer need to be imagined behind a figure
    whose absence also no longer requires imagining.

In the space opening, I remember how much I love
    this light this tree this room this house, the way back

stairs, closing behind me in the dark, become my
    grandmother's, on summer nights with voices rising,

falling from outside. I step across the landing
    to look at her bedroom lit by a cream globe that

picks out the fine shadows on her crocheted
    throw, the mirror tipped to show the doorway

empty as I peer in, blouse damp, sweat
    beading my shoulders, hands and face hot-

scented with night. I stand for a moment, years,
    re-waking to the smudged window I look past

until day, tired at last of trees, the endless
    play of sun and jade light, turns its head away

[*mauve, yellow*]: *a cento*

She complains to her three distinct, personal gods:
    eyes, lips, dreams. No one. The sky and the road.

To be whole and lonely again, the tongue tries to
    go back down the throat, wallpapered with cries

of birds: astonished whites and reds. And when
    it seems possible to disappear into someone,

absence takes the shape of beaten snow,
    sleep without laughter, vines twisted into

different kinds of silence – gray, vagrant,
    the color of cold sky, wind the size of a wrist.

A body wants to be held and held and
    what can you do about that? One day she will

fall through herself like an anvil, a girl's comb,
    a feather, into a world where even words grow

thin and transparent, like pale wings of ants
    that fly out of the oldest houses. Slowly

she will become a light summer dress,
    a random mauve or yellow that celebrates

nothing except mauve or yellow, as if no one
    is ever at home inside a name. Without a name

the body can be anyone's, a small bitter seed of
    tongue, a world uninhabited, without visitors,

beams and window glass letting go of themselves.

[*downtown auroras*]

> Aurora, IL, was the first city in the United States
> to use electricity for publicly lighting the entire
> City, and became known as the "City of Lights."

Thirty years from my last glance past
    these intersected lights,

street still wraps a library (white slabbed,
black-slit windows) then crosses

a river laced with silt and metal-
                yellow foam.

An overpass buckles as it lifts a railroad:
street rolls east, then slows on a hill

where light stutters, hums, comes on
    over women who posed

in strident-tight polyester. Beneath the bridge
galled acid-green, from slant-lit water

they resurface one by one: faceless man-
nequins in gaudy halters, bared legs.

On a corner, a closed parasol edged with lemon
ruffle twirls, changes hands, twirls again.

    *

Voices, unfaced: an uncle home
from the war, my aunt running just ahead

of the sun toward a streetcar that takes
her to a linens counter downtown.

Blue-leaved trees tunnel over the street-
car as it passes the yard where I will live, new-

planted with apple, roses, crocuses.
In houses next door, Florence and Agnes are still

middle-aged, Mrs. Richards not yet a widow.
At dusk, my grandfather's half-filled beer glass

shivers as my aunt slams the screen, flushed,
her gloves forgotten on the trolley seat, again.

    *

A chain lifts, link after link, past a window
      falling through water in first,

curtained light. October blue fills
the shape of a wooden yellow bird

perched on a closet door. Hours stay empty
and open: think of an aster's green

brittle fist loosening. Small losses
the size of a cedar chest (a room, a house)

    drift seaward, coral
beads sewn on a finger seam, the torn

hem of a dress, where a tucked letter ends
asking, asking...*and how are you?*

[what is locked out wants everything back]: a cento

From the cicada lace of my body
steps a ceramic woman with a row of birds
for hair, her face a tapestry hung from beaks.

Clouds catch and pass over glass-skinned
hands, her feet peonies licked open by ants.
She is not the mouth of anything I write
                    these days

that begin with a stutter of sun, then rain.
She stands on my dresser before a small
wooden crowd, speaking the language

of carved earth, stone. Like a silver-backed
river or snake, she steps constantly
new from her shed moment into its altared

perception. I wake each dawn to watch where
            she falls, learning how
day finds its twin: one black and one blood.

[*when i wake it will be forever*]

Silence minus amazement: generous
holes hidden in high stony
fields overhang the sea, slow swim back

toward the center of a bed no longer
shared, a body's definition
of all its lost parts, gold and foliate:

hummingbird – 1. *rooted in the palm; shaped*
to the curve of each temple   2. *shimmer-green*
hearing   3. *throat flutter evolving to whir.*

A man's shade the flat white of a village wall
wraps vineyards turned
to vinegar, damp violets underfoot littered

with plums – pits like tin-gray lithographs
printed from gabbro and basalt,
ballast for the serpentine, blue-foil grass:

viper's bugloss – 1. *rough hair protruding, blue-*
stung   2. *found in bare-waste places; between spread*
hands   3. *red-stamen fingers thorning green air.*

A foyer steeped in lemon-orange zest, ginger
steps past a window filled with sundown
whistle, acrid as a fifth, shrill chamber of heart,

small talons caught on shed-skin words,
thrum of plum blossoms long-
fallen: sightless, scentless, hydrangea-raged.

[blonde and sad skeletons, whistle, whistle]

Through glass, map a world without sound: wine
blue, lime-russet trees draping yellow concrete – primary,

tangible. Death continues with brisk affection
and red galls, leaf-tips lit like nerve endings.

Summer, I am leaving now, before night arrives
and starts throwing its weight around. Past the fence

laced in cicada shells, chrysanthemums curl
like a chrysalis for December's thirty-one torn skins.

Autumn laps gently as a well-fed dog: each pale
branch remembers leaves as essential things,

and how easy it is to let things go. Voice gathers in
the gap of breath just starting to sharpen, one end

tucked under another, woven and unwearable.
Green leaf, red leaf, green again. Only August,
                                                    and already falling.

[*the age we live in*]

By virtue of being a woman alone,
there are men who assume interest

on my part must be personal and
      sexual. This is not true

of all men – only those I have met: or not met:
      or smiled at: or passed in the street.

A free-floating assumption, I know, adrift
beneath words, making it almost a favor

when a man I was partnered with
at a conference introduced himself
as *very, very married*, giving me a chance

      to relieve him directly
by declaring myself *very, very lesbian*:

a thin-bright, only slightly bitter lie,
and nothing like real desire, which is more
      violent: unswerving: rare.

      You are here now,
face hidden in hands, refusing again

to believe in a beginning that keeps bringing
      us back to this point

of leaving: my leaving, yours. I tell you to
step into this moment, toward another

and another, toward me, but the truth is
you will make of me what you can, and I
      have to let you

return to before I existed, real desire wanting real
      erasure: days months years

I have stood nearly fifty in this body,
      long enough

to grow unashamed of want without trying
to make an art of it. Long enough to know
      what I have: each night

II

If I did not exist, you might
step through me, past your

self, a hundred times a day
never wondering who I was.

[*one voice may survive the other*]

The poem means to become more than it is.
      Broken. Incorporated. Indistinguishable.

The poem waits endlessly to begin again.
      The poem wants fathers – as many as it can get.

Fathers who believe the poem
      will save them. Fathers enthralled.

The poem does not want mothers –
      mothers who know the poem saves nothing

and have already contained its voice.
      A line is an outward and visible sign of silence

wanting to break: the poem is a promise
      to at least make a good story of it, and to keep

the story the poem's own. Silence circles
      a bared space where the poem slowly unfolds.

The poem wants to waken all voice,
      all placed edge to edge. Wary. Aware.

Each secretly wishing to fall still.
      Each longing to go on. The poem open to both.

[i am named]

I am named for the Virgin Mary and my aunt   ~~that generosity~~
who died while my mother was pregnant. By suicide.   ~~is essential~~
Unclear: dead by suicide, or pregnant   ~~in this world~~
by suicide? Suicidal pregnancy? Don't ask me   ~~and rare~~

or my three-year-old sister who kept parroting
why did she do it why did she do it
all the way to grandmother's house, while my mother
was put to bed in the dark. Don't ask me, little girl,

this is all I know: that I'm named for the mother   ~~that joy~~
of a god and an aunt who died, pregnant with suicide: ~~is our birthright~~
that later my mother would wonder aloud *why*   ~~as misery~~
do you remind me of her? Don't ask me, mom,   ~~is our condition~~

I wasn't there and nearly never here, and always
keep death the god of all possible options, even when
pregnant. At thirteen, I held my breath for five years
but my mother only said, *don't ask me,*

come up with your own story, all mine are   ~~that absence~~
back in the ground: pregnant with death, by death.   ~~is a generous~~
The earth is also a way out, silence is also a   ~~long-lived~~
part of speech, but don't ask me –   ~~if~~----------

each buried secret says the same thing, if you listen.

[red wanders to red]: *a cento*

Red wanders to red, like poppies and
    memory. It steps toward me on steady feet,

gives me a veil. "Take this for dreaming,"
    says its stitchery. More than the dove,

more than the mulberry, Autumn nibbles its leaf
    from my hand, wearing rings that are rusting.

What's dead put its arms around you too –
    hushed tongues that don't split off No from Yes,

so that a mouth might thirst for this later:
    voices veined with night, vibrating consonants,

ropes we hang the bell on. Unseen cathedrals,
    rivers unheard, clocks deep in us are all hands,

like russet thorntrees in blossom
    in gorselight – hands we try teaching to sleep.

Muteness is roomy, a house that ticks toward us,
    a green silence, a sepal. I lie beside you, empty,

audible, our conversation daygray.
    There is earth inside words that bloom red –

like slender dog roses they break loose,
    they float. We speak with blinded mouths,

seagreen needles stitching the split. I leaf
    you open, uncurling each word from snow.

[city ringed with erased roads]

A gray-lipped man circles a pond, hands bare
and raw. Our concern is rehearsed, blue-

rounded and rushed, but still *meant,*
intending to mean, just as his words are

earnest, leaning toward, and already lost
    in speaking – leaving us

bodies alone to put on, take off, voice
spun into spray across water. Beneath junipers,

two stick figures drawn as with a brush
handle through paint: one kneels,

    arms angled toward the other
staring back down rifle-sights, lines lost

in the nod and sway of limbed shade.
The city creeps near, with its windows turned off.

    Shadows lie in the alley –
who do they belong to? Perhaps just laundry

hanging from balconies, but the shadows
don't know they're from shirts, and they flutter

    sad wrists with no hands,
headless necks, the air violet with early spring.

[poppy red]

A soldier in World War I brings
    a German bride back to America,

but he does not love
    women and she stays locked

her whole married life in a
    language she cannot learn.

There are children who leave and don't
    come back, even when the mother dies

and the father's health fails. *What kind*
    of children are these? people ask, who

still consider the husband a kind man –
    remember, the wife spoke only silence.

What kind of children? you ask, and I
    look away – I have already shared

what I know, and there is nothing one
    will not do to another, again and again.

[my grandmother stands]

Circled in smoke on her porch,
she explains her names were given
in the wrong order, Hazel being

fit only for a middle initial –
she always intended to be Violet.
Framed by a street curved

over with tree boughs, her wide lawn
makes the porch not just a cool
blue detail, but a necessary shade.

Nails and mouth glow red, upswept
hair a flat black that reflects
no light, her starched yellow smock

trellised with roses the size of saucers
and rumor. *Now Violet,* she declares,
is a name you can work with. Friends

could call me Vi – everyone would.
Except my beaus. Said with a snap
of her cigarette case. *They would have to*

call me Violet. And here she might
soften with a smile, a shake of the head,
but instead she disappears

into the house, the searing heat,
a few rubied stubs scattered over grass.

[*middle school as a famished, half-frozen dog*]

Class after class, wind answers itself
in the brittle leaf shells curled on branches.

I am nowhere and worried, watching snow
tear the afternoon to pieces large enough

to bury a sleeve, a drawn hood.
I want to step into now or that or blue:

that blue: blue now: a face painted, laced,
erased. In the hall, Mr. Adal dances

in drag to demonstrate Carnival: a moment
unpacked from home in the Canary Islands.

I'd be scared to do that, says a twelve-year-old
boy, looking. Outside, a father folds snow-

thick arms, grinning *beautiful, beautiful*
to the sky, while silhouettes shimmy behind

iced glass. The new red is red again –
clawed raw, tubed. Nails and peep-toes, too.

[tongue]: a mirror cento

i

We are no longer children   not even a shadow
   of a child   Soon we'll no longer be possible

Inside my forehead an insect ticks – time is
   born in me   Fullness   without taste scent sound

breath   its wings brown-red   veined
   Behind each wing-tip   a little spine   band of pearls

glowing in blue   singing through the innermost
   skin   Every word carries   the whole universe

Birth is enormous   My own language isn't
   empty enough   I dissolve from within   No labyrinth's

web is opening   As if I did not exist   from the
   darkness of my throat I rise   like mist over sand

like shadow on glass hands curved
   around a colorless bud   stone   polished by sea

ii

We are a city aged clearly into itself   beyond
     abandoned   beyond restoration   I wake in a room

overlooking gray ocean where   a woman swims
     into wave   She is becoming sea-

smooth   rinsed with foam   her birth-
     scarred body   scoured by song   into shore

In the courtyard words fountain, fall   unobscured
     by a blur of water   We are a city   so completely

ruined our star-worn sky splits   spilling shadow
     into a center emptied   enough to receive it   like red

wind curving   lips of drifted roads   Like a glass-
     paneled door   slipped from its latch   swinging in

salted dawn   lifts each   square of crumpled
     light from a bed   to scatter   like seed over sand

[about dying and then not]

A tree downed by a storm
    lies on its side for years,

half dead, the other still
    leafing out each spring,

and already it is something
    other than a tree – my daughter

examines snapped rootlets
    strung with tiny mushrooms

and shudders while she traces
    from a distance each gray branch

that twines new green.
    It fell the year we discovered

a suicide here and pulled him
    out of his locked, running car

and held his head to pick
    broken glass from his hair

while waiting for the ambulance,
    which came late, without lights

or sirens, and to fill the silence
    I told him everything I knew

about dying and then not –
    of course, for all his flutter

and startles, I might have been
    talking to a corpse not yet aware

it was at the end of experience.
    I want to share and not say

all the details that still litter
    this shoulder, to remember how

intimate death is, how we were
    not invited into his but stumbled

on it by chance, the tree still up-
    right and only itself, my daughter

already stepping back – apart, appalled.

[a protean geography] i

A woman enters an ocean and stretches,
grows immense in the swells, bridging coast
      with coast. Is she still

her body? an icon? the sea? Our new definition
for *water* or *shoreline*: soft salt lift-lilt fall.

Red ribbons an oak branch, becomes lizard-
skitter over stone, garnet coiling a wrist.
      No, it is blue-

ringed with two clear-facet centers: gannet
eyes a world stares through, swallowed
      so long ago it is now

impossible to remove. Listen: beneath skin
the hiss of a thousand cities' glass-rinsed shores,

      every step an intention
not to fall through earth, each face passed
a handful of questions we keep planting in sand:

      come closer; stay
    distant; I am going somewhere
      you can't follow.

Planted and watered with sea, we watch sky come
unpinned and lower its braids to us,
clasp them round our wrists and begin to climb.

III Curiosity Boxes

Comes I as [frame]
[contained] a mask

splitting *we* into *that*
and calling it [they]

*Curiosity Boxes are based on the concept of boxed assemblages, such
as those created by the artist Joseph Cornell.*

[*i*]

Silhouettes cut from hot night
slipped behind a porch rail,

overhead a sky of one star:
blue stone set above a tree

leafed into the shape of a skull.
Enameled planes blink

in the tree's blank eye: bodies
disappear into other bodies.

A low, red note swings upward,
tracing language dissolved

in the thirst of midday. Out-
lines hold night close, clothed

in what the sun leaves behind.

[*ii*]

It is the best
worst place:

children too
quiet, state-

of-the-art di-
agnostics, hall-

ways for each
parent to pace,

convinced that
a terrible error

has occurred.
Few escape

on their own
two feet and

the box never
seems emptier.

[*iii*]

A teacup, round body
that blues light shining

through, shaped to fit
with a click in a saucer

lost years ago: given
to a woman whose

husband has just died:
left in a garden, holding

an earthworm, two
earwigs: rinsed clean

to float a cut lily, a rose:
ringed with an enameled

gold band or kept plain
and chipped, because all

she wants is to break
dish after dish after dish.

[*iv*]

Empty dinner plates, clay
women scattered among them:

press a button and hear one
complain of a sore shoulder

injured, healed and hurting
again – press twice for a hum

of sympathetic suggestions,
her sadness a continuous loop

of agitation. Press again: figures
rise, gather hats, coats, biscuit

tins, one moving slower, bent
stiff over sleeves and boots,

another at the door repeating
how good it was to see her and

to take care as she goes, the steps
being dark and covered in ice.

[*v*]

Three windows split the back
frame into strips of smoke-

blue and corn fields half stubble,
half husk: between glass a bare

pool deck covered in Sunday
dust. Not Hopperesque, but a real

place to ask Edward in and see
what he can brush from this space:

the empty that is here and hidden.

[*vi*]

Rain rigged to drip from two
top wooden corners: staccato

blur without words. A porch
swing hangs at the center,

glows orange in green-water
air. A dreamed body wanting

    to wake, the dream
wanting to go on, searches,

wings bruised against glass,
broken sleep, motionless swing.

[*vii*]

Slits in paper covering glass
back-lit by blue neon:

glimpse of a waiting room
where silhouettes adjust hats

and leave, their lack of face
lifting them from themselves.

[*viii*   ]

On the sleet-side of a train
window, cars stall at crossings,

figures pool under salt-orange
street lamps. Towns flicker,

go dark. Inside the carriage
one face stares out, another

looks back, reflected, multiple.
A man hurries past the empty

seats, past cups, gloves, papers,
a cap, and then not even that.

IV

Came I, I, I, and I.
Came *until* *instead*

and proclaimed Now
as a restless press

from inside, a pushing:
and and and

[*signs you're losing your vision*]

Yellow-walled hours collapse into calm
alarm, like hands placed, palm-up, in a worn
linen lap. Today I have died so little,
stepping lightly over ground that unlaces

decades. Streets careen with vertigo,
alleys restless with shade: no one
as they used to be. Gold gone
gray-hazed, like five o'clock air, slant red

cries of exhausted children, all their stories
displaced. What world is this, dim foot-
falls of a half-formed thought missing each

third step, without the precision of music
or cruelty? A mountain shifts an attic shelf:
be ready to seize the ordinary and leap clear.

[viper's bugloss] i

Sweet Jesus, I found you
by the side of the road –
broken, naked and cold.
I held you and warmed you,
bathed you and clothed you,
and then I let you go.

(Refrain)
Sweet, sweet Jesus my Savior,
there by the side of the road!
I found you and held you,
bathed you and clothed you,
and then I let you go.

Try to become a god curled beside
a rose quartz wall that took three
years to build, stone scavenged
from woods, abandoned fields.

Try to release breath circled by rib-
clasped, elaborate labyrinths,
hollow bone-lace prone
to snapping, sky-stained lips.

Try to nod like the blue-bent
heads rooting beneath skull
and thorn-threaded fingers, toes:
sing thistle mouth, bride's whistle,

two faces framed in a widowed
house, each pane a cropped view:
first the foundling, washed
and wrapped, then the letting go.

[*dreams layered with babies*]

New bodies slip into sleep
    each night: babies mis-

placed, forgotten, slight
    yellow birds the weight of

an afterthought perched
    on my pillow at dawn,

willing to be caged by
    hands, fine wire beneath

feathered skin thrown
    back to air – one newborn

jumps up, gingerbread run-
    ning between houseless

windows – floating panes
    jeweled red and green, until

he is lost in glass scoured
    clear, sealed into prisms of

leaded bevel – another blue
    infant laid in the washing

machine in seamless dream
    logic broken by the spin cycle –

a low-ceilinged house, rows
    and rooms of small drawers

lined with silk, ready for
    newborns that arrive limp,

naked, gray – I wash and
    swaddle them into boxes –

sound and sleeping as long as I
    sleep, waiting for them to wake.

[down by the water]

My daughter is afraid of ghosts
    I can't see. *Show me*, I say –

she points to the staircase
    where a small girl appears,

wet, edging round the room
    until I cross over and lift her up,

soaking the front of my blouse.
    She is thirsty so I give her

water that streams through
    sheer skin and gathers in pools

as I carry her to the door.
    What she wants is to go back

to the sea, so I take her
    in cold rain to the river, step in,

and let go. For a moment
    I imagine light tugs at my ankles,

myself afraid, before
    fingers loosen and wash away.

In the house it is quiet, then a
    thud from upstairs, a scraping step.

What's that, I ask – my daughter
    answers, *Now comes the mom.*

[*i sleep in the hand that breaks the clocks*]: *a cento*

Full-settled, as in red mirror moons,
    my dead do not transcend the tomb.

I ask my son, "When is my day?"
    and he answers, "Your day is coming soon."

Slowly the world between my eyelashes rises,
    tidings from the final sea, a roof of bottles

that dreams the sailor's memory.
    I dream of my children: a silk thread

wraps me, and each of their kisses,
    with a turn, unravels me. Tenderly,

they entomb birds in an empty spool-box,
    dried-apple cadavers that speak our tongue.

    When is my day?
        They laugh, *Soon, soon.*

In the hand that breaks the clocks
    I sleep full-settled as red mirror moons.

Crows become planets and sprout grass
    feathers, leaves falling from their throats,

worlds and wheels repeating themselves.
    After nights of breathless ruby, I become

what waits at the end of the tunnel,
    dawn's stubborn lens tracing each

thing's hurry away from its name,
    the receding sea baring day's new teeth.

[*witches broom*]

A moth large as a house alights,
feet barely brushing shingles,

its new-dried green the exact
color of summers one never expects
     to see again.

I want more than you
offer, something austere –

slight lamp-sway through woods,
a red-hooded jacket worn,

adored years ago that casts
a glow, panes loosening the wind:

    come in   come in.
Am I beautiful yet? Be careful

of what you are willing to do
without: children covered with

cobwebs, windows that hang in air,
a forest of candied cottages,

pale animals caught in a fell
of bluets and witches broom.
    Each season

built this wall, your body
rushing away from the names
    I gave you.

Cracks in the plaster become
a fascination, as when a crazing

of bare oak branches against
night sky becomes openings,

an escape from the predatory
eyes trapped in moth wings

that warn *I am not what I seem
and no one will thank me for it.*

[*the walls of the house*]

Covered with touches of the old
woman who lost her sight

and counted stairs, trailing
fingers along the halls before

taken out of reach. As always,
there is no happy ending:

the walls never felt her marks
that are still here, painted over.

    *

The walls of the house are old
and blind: they remember

only the smell of cat, lathed plaster,
fieldstone cellar breathing cool air.

Each year stoops closer to the ground
and the walls know nothing about it:

only at night, in winter, a shift
and crack that is almost complaint.

    *

The walls of the house test
and stretch their bones, ready

to rise up, grab a cane, and go tapping
all the doors and windows in town.

[glass violin]: a cento

      I want a glass violin
crafted from a world too naked,
                       too embraced,

too lost in the stretch of grave
up to its blue skull to see music

precise as a beetle that lies on the path
through wheat grass and mint,
three pairs of legs folded neatly on its belly.

Earth eats and breathes air, and sleeps,
clothed in skin and blood just beneath,
and people who live with practical claws,

a failing of infant fingernails, not knowing
that bell ropes, like human hair, turn gray.

      Mirrors here
are cruel and smooth as asphalt: all of us
fit neatly inside the empty envelope
propped against a cup by the suicide's bed.

Questions: under what conditions
do you dream of the dead?

What do they hold in their hands?
And in their eyes, what do you see?
                     Be specific.

Statistics: of all loves, mention only marriages;
of all children, only those who were born;

from each hundred, those not to be taken
    lightly: forty and four.

In the garden, someone digs up a rusted
argument from beneath a bush,

someone crouches under a bench,
pretending to be a wolf,
just like the growling we call a dog.

As if only a room away, the world sings
and combs her hair, which still grows.

[a protean geography] ii

A mountain is given an impossible
task: to rock on all fours like a woman
giving birth. Upheaval of an entire

    being. It is not a place
possible to avoid: you are already here.
A car with men in dark glasses

running beside it drives under a bridge
and never comes out, though the men do,
framing the space where the car had been.

Adjust your hands to another,
newly cropped view: there will be no child.
The absence of child is also an image.

A woman stands straight, naked, and breaks
the skyline, a city unmoored at her feet –
stone houses drowned, wrists a thin spire.

She is beautiful, as all women are beautiful
in the way they are not you, and the way
    they are. As a labor:

an abandon: a city's torn shore and unsettled
sleep skirting the edge of someone else,
    a cup holding all our suns.

[viper's bugloss] ii

Across the graveyard, catawba trunks become
pillars the autumn sun shines through,
lamp-lit eyes in a house we will never enter,
                                                  though we almost

hear music, feel shadows thrown from inside
pass over our body, padded against cold. Why
here, picking our way among boxed bones?
                                                  Why this light?

Why not squeezed in a desert market
spiced with heat, bodies not our own?
Or a temple faced with statues and lime-
                                                  stone stairs worn

down and down? In the center, a court-
yard planted with saltcedar, an abandoned
cistern: at bottom, another box of small
                                                  bones, forgotten

before the death of the one who lowered
them in. I give them back to you now,
along with the clipped November dusk
                                                  and this other earth,

swept bare and set with ancient, water-
carved columns, each fingertip holding day's
last heat: a waste ground spiked with viper's
                                                  bugloss, thorn-tongue

leaves ringing blooms that glow salmon-
blue in a slant-sun that doesn't lift or dip,
but stays here and here and here –
                                                  flower mouths open,

frilled, hungry birds that learn endurance
under clouds raveling from clove-smoke censers
swung in a rented procession of no one
                              who asks where we're from.

[for you I have no comforting words]: a cento

You and that other you and that other one, you won't get away —
    between yesterday and tomorrow we swing together.

Be silent with me, as all bells are silent. How often I thought that I:
    could be you as well: split apart and go on. Now I lean forward,

slip into your shadow at night. Make sure you stay awake!
    I want to lie with you and not betray you. There is rain,

rain in this house, the blind flight of bats — who lives here?
    Who drifts off with the dawn, a ghost lit by other ghosts?

Each new day wants to be longer, scented with early green apples.
    I've tried to be a stranger on this earth, and I don't want

to have faith in myself alone anymore, some leaf-like thing
    that floats between earth and sky and never lands on the ground.

Only autumn stares at us this way, with such a yellow lynx-gaze.
    Soon, snow will blow in, like a wolf chasing a herd of wild swans,

toward you and you and that other you — never anyone but you.

[*i will not become what i mean to you*]

You fall in love with the suicide
in my voice and I slowly go still –

words ripple, unreadable, out of reach.
Evening arrives limp with ice-melt, skin

gloves unlaced, serrated phrases
tucked under the mattress,

keyholes filled with silver and all
    our gold plate.

At moonrise, my shadow becomes a bear.
Shoulder bones row under fur,

screened laughter drifts over streets,
mixed with the flinched scatter
    of badger, fox, wolf –

coyotes the most awful because
they are most afraid: they give up,
    again and again

each scream caught by the throat as you
    wake, watching

a car slide toward the ravine,
    the friend step off a ledge,
        a baby slip through the rail –

everything that will not outlive the night.

Shadow floods a house filled with
children, my children sleeping inside.

A shared belief: that our greatest
challenge is to survive one another.

A common error: to assume the silence
        will last.

Everything is fine here and yes,
            I still write. Take care —

NOTES

[*a world scarcely the size of an apple*] A cento using lines, including the title, from various translated poems of Pablo Neruda.

[*the tree across the street*] The last couplet is based on the final lines of "The Last Words of My English Grandmother," by William Carlos Williams.

[*mauve, yellow*] A cento using lines from various poems by Larry Levis.

[*downtown auroras*] The epigraph is taken from the Aurora, IL website.

[*what is locked out wants everything back*] A cento using lines, including the title, from various poems by Simone Muench and Ed Roberson.

[*blonde and sad skeletons, whistle, whistle*] The title and the lines "*Summer, I am leaving now,*" and "*December's thirty-one torn skins,*" are variations on lines translated from the poems of César Vallejo.

[*red wanders to red*] A cento using lines, including the title, from various translated poems of Paul Celan.

[*city ringed with erased roads*] The title is a variation on a line from Octavio Paz. The following lines are based on images, but not necessarily the exact language, found in various translated works of the noted poets:
the city creeps near, with its windows turned off – Tomas Tranströmer
shadows lie in the alley – who do they belong to? – Alejandro
        Jodorowsky
perhaps just laundry hanging from balconies, but the shadows don't know they're from shirts – Fernando Pessoa

[*tongue*] Section i. is a cento using lines from various translated poems of Göran Sonnevi.

[*signs you're losing your vision*] The line "*today I have died so little,*" is taken from the translated poems of César Vallejo.

[*down by the water*] The title is taken from PJ Harvey's song of the same name (Universal Music, 1995.)

[*i sleep in the hand that breaks the clocks*] A cento using lines, including the title, translated from various Spanish-language poems.

[*glass violin*] A cento using lines from various translated poems of Wisława Szymborska.

[*protean geography*]*ii* The line, "*Upheaval of an entire being,*" is a variation of a translated line from Marcel Proust's *Sodom and Gomorrah.*

[*for you i have no comforting words*] A cento using lines, including the title, from various translated poems of Ingeborg Bachmann, Sándor Csoóri, and Robert Desnos.

[*i will not become what i mean to you*] The title is taken from Barbara Kruger's 1983 gelatin silver print, "*We Will Not Become What We Mean to You.*"

ABOUT THE AUTHOR

Virginia Smith Rice earned her MFA in Creative Writing from Northwestern University, where she received the Distinguished Thesis Award for her poetry manuscript, *One Voice May Survive the Other*.

She currently lives in Woodstock, IL where she works as an art teacher. She is also co-editor of the online poetry journal, *Kettle Blue Review*.

SUNDRESS PUBLICATIONS TITLES

The Lost Animals
David Cazden
$14.00 ISBN 978-1-939675-07-1

A House of Many Windows
Donna Vorreyer
$14.00 ISBN 978-1-939675-05-7

Gathered: Contemporary Quaker Poets
Ed. by Nick McRae
$16.00 ISBN 978-1-939675-01-9

The Hardship Post
Jehanne Dubrow
$14.00 ISBN 978-1-939675-03-3

Too Animal, Not Enough Machine
Christine Jessica Margaret Reilly
$10.00 ISBN 978-1-939675-02-6

The Old Cities
Marcel Brouwers
$14.00 ISBN 0-9723224-9-3

One Perfect Bird
Letitia Trent
$14.95 ISBN 0-9723224-8-5

Like a Fish
Daniel Crocker
$14.95 ISBN 0-9723224-8-5

The Bone Folders
T.A. Noonan
$14.95 ISBN 0-9723224-6-9

Especially the Deer
Tyurina Allen, Mary Beth Magin,
& Julie Ruble
$12.95 ISBN 0-9723224-0-X

Printed in the USA
CPSIA information can be obtained
at www.ICGtesting.com
JSHW080310150624
64710JS00010B/46

9 781939 675101